MW01146371

PROTEVANGELIUM
OF JAMES

Edited by

JAMES ORR

LONDON: J.M. DENT & CO.: 1903
PHILADELPHIA: J.B. LIPPINCOTT CO.

Introduction

The Canonical Gospels. As far back as we can trace them the four Gospels known as Canonical hold a place of honour and authority peculiar to themselves. Irenæus of Gaul (*circa* A.D. 175) recognises four, and only four, Gospels as the 'pillars' that uphold the Church (*Adv. Haer.* iii. 8). Origen, in the beginning of the next century (A.D. 220), speaks of them as 'the four Gospels which alone are uncontroverted in the Church of God spread under heaven' (Euseb., *H. E.* vi. 25). Justin Martyr, in the middle of the second century, narrates that the 'Memoirs of the Apostles,' which are called Gospels, were read every Sunday in the assemblies of the Christians (*Apol.* 66, 67). That these Gospels were those we now possess we can tell, not only from Justin's description of them, and allusions to their contents (*cp.* Sanday's *Gospels in Second Century*, chap. iv.), but from the harmony made of them by his disciple Tatian in his *Diatessaron* (now recovered in Arabic translations). Our four Gospels, and these only, stand at the head of the ancient Syriac (*Peshitta*), the Latin and the Egyptian versions (*cp.* Westcott and Hort), and of the old list known as the Canon of Muratori (*circa* A.D. 180). Within the Church, in short, our four Gospels, attributed by second-century writers to their present authors, had never any rivals.

Apocryphal Writings. It stands very differently, as respects origin, character and reception, with the Gospels, Acts and Apocalpyses known as 'Apocryphal.' These began to be produced (so far as known) in the second century, mostly in Ebionitic and Gnostic circles, and, with few exceptions, were repudiated and condemned by the Church. Only later, and in modified and expurgated forms, did their stories pass into the general Catholic tradition. The second century seems to have been a perfect hot-bed for the production of this class of writings. The heretical *Gospel of the Egyptians* is already quoted in 2 Clement (*circa* A.D. 140). Irenæus speaks of the sect of the Marcosians as adducing 'an unspeakable number of apocryphal and spurious writings, which they themselves had forged, to bewilder the minds of the foolish,' and instances the story, found in the *Gospel of Thomas*, of Jesus confounding the schoolmaster who sought to teach Him His letters (*Adv. Haer.* i. 20). Later tradition attributed the composition of many of the apocryphal writings (*Pseudo-Matthew*, Acts of Apostles) to a mythical Leucius, a disciple of the Apostles (*cp.* art. 'Leucius,' *Dict. of Christ.*

Biog.). Eusebius gives a list of spurious and disputed books: 'That we may have it in our power to know both these books (the canonical) and those that are adduced by the heretics under the name of the Apostles, such, viz., as compose the Gospels of Peter, of Thomas, and of Matthew, and certain others beside these, or such as contain the Acts of Andrew and John, and of the other Apostles, of which no one of those writers in the ecclesiastical succession has condescended to make any mention in his works; and, indeed, the character of the style itself is very different from that of the Apostles, and the sentiments, and the purport of those things that are advanced in them, deviating as far as possible from sound orthodoxy, evidently proves they are the fictions of heretical men; whence they are not only to be ranked among the spurious writings, but are to be rejected as altogether absurd and impious' (*H. E.* iii. 25). Only a small part of this extensive literature remains to us, and in no case in its original form, but solely in later, and often much-altered recensions.

Authorities. The apocryphal literature is a study by itself, with the intricate details of which only specialists are competent to deal. Great attention has been bestowed on the collecting, editing and collating of such codices of Gospels,

Acts, and other writings as were formerly known, or have more recently been discovered. The most important of the older collections was that of Fabricius (*Codex Apocryphus*, 1719). The collections and prolegomena of Thilo (1832) and Tischendorf (*Acts*, 1851; *Gospels*, 1853; *Apocalypses*, 1856) are of special value; much, however, has been done since their time. The articles by Lipsius in the *Dict. of Christ. Biog.* on 'Acts of the Apostles (Apocryphal)' and 'Gospels (Apocryphal)' are, like the author's learned German work (2 vols., 1883) on the former subject, masterly in their discussions of the relations of the documents. Valuable light was thrown on the Syriac versions of the *Protevangelium of James*, the *Gospel of Thomas*, and the *Transitus Mariæ* (Passing of Mary), by the texts and fragments edited and translated by Dr. W. Wright in the *Journal of Sacred Literature* (January and April 1865), and his *Contributions to the Apocryphal Literature of the New Testament* (1865), and *Apocryphal Acts of the Apostles* (1871). In 1902 Mrs. Agnes Smith Lewis edited, with translations and other illustrative matter, new Syriac texts of the *Protevangelium* and *Transitus Mariæ*, obtained from a palimpsest she was fortunate enough to purchase at Suez in July 1895 (*Studia Sinaitica*, No. XI. 1902). An interesting fragment of the lost *Gospel of Peter* (second century) was discovered, with other MSS., at Akhmim, in Upper Egypt, in 1886, and was published in 1892. A translation of the Apocryphal Gospels was published in 1874 by Mr. B. H. Cowper, on the basis of Tischendorf's edition; and Vol. XVI. of Messrs. T. & T. Clark's *Ante-Nicene Library* is devoted to translations by Mr. A. Walker of 'Apocryphal Gospels, Acts and Revelations.' An 'Additional Volume' of the *Library* (1897) contains translations of works more recently discovered Lectures XI. and XIX. of Dr. Salmon's *Introduction to the New Testament*, on 'Apocryphal and Heretical Gospels' and 'Apocryphal Acts of the Apostles,' may profitably be consulted. Hone's catch-penny *Apocryphal New Testament* (1820) is critically worthless.

Character of Apocryphal Gospels. Of the purely heretical Gospels most have perished (for an account of some of the Gnostic ones, *see* Baring-Gould's *Lost and Hostile Gospels* (1874), and Lipsius, as above). But apart from doctrinal reasons, sufficient motive always existed in persons of lax tendency to pander to the principle of curiosity and love of the marvellous in human nature by inventions of narratives on subjects on which the genuine Gospels were silent. An existing narrative, or traditions of sayings and doings of Jesus, might be, and frequently were, manipulated, recast, or embellished; but the grand opportunity came when the Gospels said nothing at all. Here was a space which imagination could fill up at pleasure. The stories might be puerile, demoralising, ridiculous to the last degree, but if they were only circumstantial and marvellous enough, and were backed up by names of Apostles, or others of repute, the narrator could always rely on finding readers greedy to receive them. This is precisely what happened with the Apocryphal Gospels. There are differences in degree of puerility and extravagance; but Bishop Ellicott did not exaggerate when he said of the spurious Gospels as a whole (and the same remarks apply as a rule to the Acts): 'Their real demerits, their mendacities, their absurdities, their coarseness, the barbarities of their style and the inconsequence of their narratives, have never been excused or condoned. It would be hard to find any competent writer, in any age of the Church, who has been beguiled into saying anything civil or commendatory' ('On the Apocryphal Gospels,' *Cambridge Essays*, 1856, p. 153). It is to be remembered, on the other hand, that the stories in these Gospels did ultimately very deeply influence Catholic tradition.

Cycles of Narration. The stories in the Apocryphal Gospels will be found on examination to resolve themselves mainly into three groups, or to form three chief cycles, corresponding to those parts of the evangelical narrative where curiosity is most excited, and receives least satisfaction. These cycles relate (1) to the previous history of the parents of Jesus, especially of Mary, and to the Nativity; (2) to the boyhood of Jesus from His childhood to His twelfth year; and (3) to the passion of Jesus, and the interval between His death and Resurrection.

A few words may be said on the cycles generally before passing to the special introduction.

1. Cycle on the Parents of Jesus and on the Nativity. Joseph and Mary are somewhat abruptly introduced in the genuine Gospels, while a long preliminary history is given in Luke of Zacharias and Elizabeth, the parents of John the Baptist. This was plainly something to be remedied, and the oldest cycle of stories, apparently without a scintilla of real tradition behind them, relate to the parentage and birth of the Virgin Mary, the wonderful circumstances of her early life, her betrothal to Joseph, the Annunciation, and the events of the Nativity. The stories grow in detail and in wonderful character as they advance from the *Protevangelium of James* (the oldest), through the *Gospel of Pseudo-Matthew,* to a third piece, *The Nativity of Mary.* But the main outlines of the narrative are early fixed. They include such features as the following:—How Mary's parents, Joachim and Anna, were rich, but childless; Joachim's distress at being repulsed from the Temple because he had no seed; his flight and fasting, and the grief of Anna; the angelic promise to the godly pair; the birth of Mary, and her dedication to God; the marvellous incidents of her infancy; how she lived with other virgins at the Temple from her third to her twelfth (or fourteenth) year, behaving astonishingly, and being fed by angels; how an aged guardian of her virginity was sought for, and by a Divine sign was found in Joseph, to whom, accordingly, she was betrothed; the Annunciation to Mary; Joseph's concern at her condition; the trial of Joseph and Mary by the water of jealousy at the Temple; the journey to Bethlehem, and birth of Jesus in a cave outside the city; the marvels attending the Nativity, etc. In the later versions of the legend the growing exaltation of Mary is very apparent. New stories arise also of the death of Joseph, and of the passing of the soul of Mary, and assumption of her body (*Transitus Mariæ*). Of the latter type of story one specimen is given.

2. The Boyhood of Jesus. The entire silence of the Gospel history on the early life of Jesus naturally afforded scope for invention, and the legend-mongers of the second and later centuries did not miss their opportunity. The blank in the narrative of the childhood and youth of Jesus was early filled up with an abundance of prodigies of the crudest and most puerile kind. The parent of this class of Gospel, or rather the earliest form of it, was the so-called *Gospel of Thomas*, which had its successors in the *Gospel of Pseudo-Matthew*, and, still later, in the wildly-extravagant *Arabic Gospel of the Infancy*. The absurdity of the sayings and doings attributed to the boy Jesus in this cycle of stories is only equalled by their grotesque incongruity with His real character. The single effect of placing them alongside the narratives of the genuine Gospels must be, as Dr. Westcott has said, to impress the reader with the sense of 'complete contrast.' Time, place, propriety, even ordinary consistency, are recklessly disregarded. Jesus has and exercises from His cradle all Divine powers—is omniscient, omnipotent, etc.—yet plays with the children in the street, and amuses Himself by making pools of water and moulding clay sparrows. When challenged for breaking the Sabbath, He claps His hands and His sparrows fly away. He is the terror of the places in which

He resides. If boy or man offends, or contradicts Him, He smites the offender dead, or otherwise avenges Himself. He confounds His teachers, and instructs them in the mysteries of the Hebrew letters. When His pitcher breaks, He carries home the water in His lap. He aids Joseph in his carpentry by lengthening or shortening the pieces of wood at pleasure. The *Gospel of Pseudo-Matthew* gives a special series of miracles wrought by Jesus as a child in Egypt (chaps. xvii. to xxv. These chapters only are included in this volume). The *Arabic Gospel of the Infancy* gives the rein to fancy in stories of marvels and transformations, which, in their bizarre extravagance, remind of nothing so much as of the *Arabian Nights.*

3. Cycle of Pilate and Nicodemus. The evangelists give full narratives of the events of the betrayal, trial, Crucifixion, and Resurrection of Jesus. The excuse of silence, therefore, cannot be pleaded here. The apocryphal narrators, however, saw room for embellishment, expansion, and sometimes modification. Later, apparently within the Catholic Church itself, they produced a series of fictitious writings, bearing on the parts taken by Pilate, Nicodemus, Joseph of Arimathea and others, in these scenes of the Saviour's suffering and triumph. First came a number of alleged letters and reports from Pilate, doubtful in date and origin, but none in their present form early. Then appeared in varying recensions the so-called *Acts of Pilate* or *Gospel of Nicodemus*, which certainly is not older than the fourth, and is possibly as late as the fifth, century. The sobriety of the Gospel histories did not satisfy the taste of these enterprising compilers. Jesus was not made to appear sufficiently Divine in his trial before the Roman procurators; Pilate's sympathy with Jesus was not sufficiently accentuated; the testimony to Christ's innocence was not thrown into bold enough relief. All this was now amended. The altercation between Pilate and Christ's accusers assumes a lengthened and highly dramatic form; Pilate avows himself unequivocally on Christ's side; the Saviour has miraculous attestation of His dignity, *e.g.*, in the Roman standards bowing down to Him as He passes with honour into the judgment hall; the persons whose healings are narrated in the Gospels—the impotent man of John 5, the woman with the issue of blood, Bartimæus, those from whom demons had been expelled, step forward and bear witness to His power. The same kind of elaboration appears in the parts taken in the history by Nicodemus and Joseph; the whole culminating in the testimony before the

Sanhedrim by eye-witnesses to the Ascension of Jesus, on receiving which Annas, Caiaphas and the Rabbis believe! A second part of the Gospel (later in origin, and not included in this selection) recounts from the lips of the two sons of Symeon, raised from the dead, the triumphs of Jesus in Hades, during the interval between His death and Resurrection.

Apocryphal Acts of the Apostles. The same motives which led to the composition of Apocryphal Gospels naturally led to the production of a multitude of spurious Acts of Apostles. These profess to narrate the journeyings, doings and teachings of the Apostles of Christ (Peter, Thomas, Andrew, Thaddæus, Matthew, etc.) after their dispersion from Jerusalem. The groundwork of several of the Acts belongs to the second century, though, in their present form, most are Catholic recastings of much later date. The *Acts of Peter and Paul*, which relate the conflicts of these Apostles with Simon Magus are of this character (in their present form probably from fourth or fifth century). The *Acts of Thomas* still bear on them the clear imprint of the Gnosticism in which they originated (second or third century). Old 'Journeyings of Peter' are wrought up in the Ebionitic *Clementine* writings (second century).

The oldest and freshest extant specimen of this class of literature is the *Acts of Paul and Thecla*, on which *see* below. The apocryphal 'Apocalypses,' of which there were a great many (of Paul, Peter, John, etc.), must here be left unnoticed. A fragment of the *Apocalypse of Peter* was discovered with the *Gospel of Peter* at Akhmim in 1886, and was published in 1902.

Something may now be said by way of more special introduction to the apocryphal work included in this volume.

1. The Protevangelium of James. This oldest of the extant Apocryphal Gospels claims to have been written by James (the Just) in Jerusalem. It was first published in the Latin version of Postellus in 1552. It exists in numerous Greek MSS., the best of which is said to be one of the tenth century. The Syriac versions are older, and, with occasional abbreviations, agree fairly with the Greek text, and with one another. The fragment translated by Dr. Wright is supposed to belong to the sixth century; the text on the palimpsest of Mrs. Lewis is referred to the fifth or sixth century. The Gospel in its present form can hardly (notwithstanding Tischendorf) be put earlier than the third century; but the older form lying behind it certainly goes back to the second century. Coincidences are noted between the

Gospel and Justin Martyr (A.D. 150) which, in the opinion of good scholars, point to its use by that apologist (*cp.* Sanday on *The Gospels in the Second Century*). Origen refers to the *Book of James* in proof that Joseph had sons by a former wife (in *Matt.* tom. x. 17); and the connection with the *Protevangelium* is not disproved by the fact that elsewhere he gives a different account of the death of Zacharias (in *Matt. Tract.* 25). The contents of the Gospel show it to have been partly based on the narratives of the Nativity in Matthew and Luke. That in its present form it is composite seems evident from chap. xviii., which is put in the first person into the mouth of Joseph, and is extravagant in its style of description. On the ground of this chapter one is tempted to suspect an origin in Essenian-Ebionitic circles. Either in its present or in an earlier shape it formed the basis of the writing afterwards to be mentioned—the *Gospel of Pseudo-Matthew*, and through it of the later *Nativity of Mary*. A prominent motive of the composer is obviously to exalt the virginity of Mary. On the errors in which the work abounds *see* the Notes.

The Protevangelium of James

*(The birth of Mary the Holy Mother of God,
and very Glorious Mother of Jesus Christ.)*[1]

The Father of Mary

IN the records of the twelve tribes of Israel was Joachim,[2] a man rich exceedingly; and he brought his offerings double, saying: There shall be of my superabundance to all the people, and there shall be the offering for my forgiveness to the Lord[3] for a propitiation for me. For the great day[4] of the Lord was at hand, and the sons of Israel were bringing their offerings. And there stood over against him Rubim,[5] saying: It is not meet for thee first to bring thine offerings,

---

[1] The title *Protevangelium* is first given in the Latin version of Postellus, 1552. The titles in the MSS. greatly vary. That adopted by Tischendorf is *The Birth of Mary the Holy Mother of God, and very glorious Mother of Jesus Christ.* James, the reputed author, is variously described as 'the Less,' 'the Lord's brother' (or 'brother of God'), 'the bishop of Jerusalem,' etc.

[2] The Church of Rome appoints March 20 as the Feast of St. Joachim. His liberality is commended in the prayers.

[3] The Syriac is clearer: 'And that portion which I owe by the law I offer it to the Lord, that it may be to me for expiation.'

[4] In the *Nativity of Mary*, the 'great day' is called 'the Festival of the Dedication' (*cp.* John 10:22). More probably the Feast of Tabernacles is meant.

[5] Better, 'Ruben' (Reuben), as in some MSS., and in *Pseudo-Matthew. Cp.* chap. vi. In the *Nativity of Mary* the priest is called 'Issachar,' and this is followed in the Mystery Plays (*Ysakar*).

because thou hast not made seed in Israel. And Joachim was exceedingly grieved, and went away to the registers of the twelve tribes[6] of the people, saying: I shall see the registers of the twelve tribes of Israel, as to whether I alone have not made seed in Israel. And he searched, and found that all the righteous had raised up seed in Israel. And he called to mind the patriarch Abraham, that in the last day[7] God gave him a son Isaac. And Joachim was exceedingly grieved, and did not come into the presence of his wife; but he retired to the desert, and there pitched his tent, and[8] fasted forty days and forty nights, saying in himself:[9] I will not go down either for food or for drink until the Lord my God shall look upon me, and prayer shall be my food and drink.

Sorrow of Anna and Joachim

---

[6] 'Registers of the twelve tribes.' The Greek word is *dodekaphulon*, and some interpret—'to the twelve tribes' (of the people). So also Syriac. But the context implies a search of records. *Cp.* l. 1, 'In the records (genealogies) of the twelve tribes of Israel.'

[7] Another reading is, 'in his last days.'

[8] *Pseudo-Matthew* says, 'He went to his flocks, taking with him his shepherds into the mountains into a far country, so that for five months his wife Anna could hear no tidings of him' (chap. ii.).

[9] 'Forty days and forty nights.' *Cp.* Exod. 24:18, 34:28; Deut. 9:9; 1 Kings 19:8; Matt. 4:2.

2. And his wife Anna mourned in two mournings,[10] and lamented in two lamentations, saying: I shall bewail my widowhood; I shall bewail my childlessness. And the great day of the Lord was at hand;[11] and Judith her maid-servant said: How long dost thou humiliate thy soul? Behold, the great day of the Lord is at hand, and it is unlawful for thee to mourn. But take this head-band,[12] which the woman that made it gave to me; for it is not proper that I should wear it, because I am a maid-servant, and it has a royal appearance.[13] And Anna said: Depart from me; for I have not done such things, and the Lord has brought me very low. I fear that some wicked person has given it to thee, and thou hast come to make me a sharer in thy sin. And Judith said: Why should I curse thee,[14] seeing that the Lord hath shut thy womb, so as not to give thee fruit in Israel? And Anna was grieved exceedingly, and put off her garments of mourning, and cleaned

---

[10] The 26th of July is the Feast of St. Anna in the Church of Rome. 'Two mournings,' from the twofold cause, her widowhood and her childlessness.

[11] 'The great day.' Possibly, as Thilo conjectures, the last day of the Feast of Tabernacles (John 7:37). Anna had been mourning during the week.

[12] Rather, which a lady, a former mistress, had given her as a reward of her work. The headband was too ornamental for a servant's use.

[13] Some MSS. read, 'And thou hast a royal appearance.'

[14] Meaning, What could I wish worse for thee than thy present condition.

her head, and put on her wedding garments, and about the ninth hour went down to the garden to walk. And she saw a laurel, and sat under it, and prayed to the Lord, saying: O God of our fathers, bless me and hear my prayer, as Thou didst bless the womb of Sarah, and didst give her a son Isaac.

3. And gazing towards the heaven, she saw a sparrow's nest in the laurel, and made a lamentation in herself, saying: Alas! who begot me? and what womb produced me? because I have become a curse in the presence of the sons of Israel, and I have been reproached, and they have driven me in derision out of the temple of the Lord. Alas! to what have I been likened? I am not like the fowls of the heaven, because even the fowls of the heaven are productive before Thee, O Lord. Alas! to what have I been likened? I am not like the beasts of the earth, because even the beasts of the earth are productive before Thee, O Lord. Alas! to what have I been likened? I am not like these waters, because even these waters are productive before Thee, O Lord. Alas! to what have I been likened? I am not like this earth, because even the earth bringeth forth its fruits in season, and blesseth Thee, O Lord.

Angelic Missions to Anna and Joachim

4. And, behold, an angel of the Lord stood by, saying: Anna, Anna, the Lord hath heard thy prayer, and thou shalt conceive,[15] and shalt bring forth; and thy seed shall be spoken of in all the world. And Anna said: As the Lord my God liveth, if I beget either male or female, I will bring[16] it as a gift to the Lord my God; and it shall minister to Him in holy things all the days of its life. And, behold, two angels came, saying to her: Behold, Joachim thy husband is coming with his flocks. For an angel of the Lord went down to him, saying: Joachim, Joachim, the Lord God hath heard thy prayer. Go down hence; for, behold, thy wife Anna shall conceive. And Joachim went down and called his shepherds, saying: Bring me hither ten she-lambs without spot or blemish, and they shall be for the Lord my God; and bring me twelve tender calves, and they shall be for the priests and the elders; and a hundred goats for all the people. And, behold, Joachim came with his flocks; and Anna stood by the gate, and saw Joachim coming, and she ran and hung upon his neck, saying: Now I know that the Lord God hath blessed me exceedingly; for, behold, the widow no longer a widow, and I the childless shall

---

[15] In *Pseudo-Matthew* Anna has already conceived seed (chap. iii.).
[16] *Cp.* Hannah's dedication of Samuel (1 Sam. 1:11).

conceive. And Joachim rested the first day in his house.

Joachim's Joy

5. And on the following day he brought his offerings, saying in himself: If the Lord God has been rendered gracious to me, the plate on the priest's[17] forehead will make it manifest to me. And Joachim brought his offerings, and observed attentively the priest's plate when he went up to the altar of the Lord, and he saw no sin in himself. And Joachim said: Now I know that the Lord has been gracious unto me, and has remitted all my sins. And he went down from the temple of the Lord justified, and departed to his own house. And her months were fulfilled, and in the ninth month Anna brought forth. And she said to the midwife: What have I brought forth? and she said: A girl. And said Anna: My soul has been magnified this day. And she laid her down. And the days having been fulfilled, Anna was purified, and gave the breast to the child, and called her name Mary.

Birth and Childhood of Mary

---

[17] The plate on the priest's mitre, inscribed 'Holiness to the Lord.' A priestly *petalon* is ascribed in tradition to the Apostle John (Euseb., *H.E.* iii. 31, v. 24). There seems to have been a belief that the *petalon* gave some indication by its appearance when an impious person approached.

6. And the child grew strong day by day; and when she was six months old, her mother set her on the ground to try whether she could stand, and she walked seven steps and came into her bosom; and she snatched her up, saying: As the Lord my God liveth, thou shalt not walk on this earth until I bring thee into the temple of the Lord. And she made a sanctuary in her bed-chamber, and allowed nothing common or unclean to pass through her. And she called the undefiled daughters of the Hebrews, and they led her astray.[18] And when she was a year old, Joachim made a great feast, and invited the priests, and the scribes, and the elders, and all the people of Israel. And Joachim brought the child to the priests; and they blessed her, saying: O God of our fathers, bless this child, and give her an everlasting name to be named in all generations. And all the people said: So be it, so be it, amen. And he brought her to the chief priests; and they blessed her, saying: O God most high, look upon this child, and bless her with the utmost blessing, which shall be for ever. And her mother snatched her up, and took her into the sanctuary of her bed-chamber, and gave her the

---

[18] 'Led her astray.' If the text is not corrupt, the Greek word can only mean that the virgins seduced her (in a good sense) from the things that might interfere with her entire consecration. *Cp.* chap. vii. The Syriac is rendered, 'rejoiced with her' (Lewis).

breast. And Anna made a song to the Lord God, saying: I will sing a song to the Lord my God, for He hath looked upon me, and hath taken away the reproach of mine enemies; and the Lord hath given me the fruit of His righteousness, singular in its kind, and richly endowed before Him. Who will tell the sons of Rubim that Anna gives suck? Hear, hear, ye twelve tribes of Israel, that Anna gives suck. And she laid her to rest in the bed-chamber of her sanctuary, and went out and ministered unto them. And when the supper was ended, they went down rejoicing, and glorifying the God of Israel.

Mary taken to the Temple

7. And her months were added to the child. And the child was two years old, and Joachim said: Let us take her up to the temple of the Lord, that we may pay the vow that we have vowed, lest[19] perchance the Lord send to us, and our offering be not received. And Anna said: Let us wait for the third year, in order that the child may not seek for father or mother. And Joachim said: So let us wait. And the child was three years old, and Joachim said:[20] Invite the daughters of the Hebrews that are undefiled, and let them

---

[19] Lest the Lord send some mark of His displeasure upon us.
[20] Virgins are again employed to prevent the child's heart from being turned aside.

take each a lamp, and let them stand with the lamps burning, that the child may not turn back, and her heart be captivated from the temple[21] of the Lord. And they did so until they went up into the temple of the Lord. And the priest received her, and kissed her, and blessed her, saying: The Lord has magnified thy name in all generations. In thee, on the last of the days, the Lord will manifest His redemption to the sons of Israel. And he set her down upon the third step of the altar, and the Lord God sent grace upon her;[22] and she danced with her feet, and all the house of Israel loved her.

Mary abides in the Temple

8. And her parents went down marvelling, and praising the Lord God, because the child had not turned back. And Mary was in the temple of the Lord as if she were a dove that dwelt there, and she received food from the hand of an

---

[21] The residence of virgins in the Temple is entirely unhistorical. *Pseudo-Matthew* and the *Nativity* elaborate the idea, and represent the Temple as an abode of a community of virgins. They remained till they were of marriageable age (*Pseudo-Matthew* iv., viii.; *Nativity* vii.)

[22] The above-named Gospels add many marvels. Mary, on being set down, runs swiftly up the fifteen steps of the Temple (corresponding to the Psalms of Degrees) without anyone helping or leading her (*Pseudo-Matthew* iv.; *Nativity* vi.)

angel.[23] And when she was twelve years old there was held a council of the priests, saying: Behold, Mary has reached the age of twelve years[24] in the temple of the Lord. What then shall we do with her, lest perchance she defile the sanctuary of the Lord? And they said to the high priest: Thou standest by the altar of the Lord; go in, and pray concerning her; and whatever the Lord shall manifest unto thee, that also will we do. And the high priest went in, taking the robe with the twelve bells into the holy of holies; and he prayed concerning her. And behold an angel of the Lord stood by him, saying unto him: Zacharias, Zacharias, go out and assemble the widowers of the people, and let them bring each his rod;[25] and to whomsoever the Lord shall show a sign, his wife shall she be. And the heralds went out through all the circuit of Judea, and the trumpet of the Lord sounded, and all ran.

---

[23] Fed by an angel. *Cp.* the (first) Latin form of the *Transitus;* 'I always guarded thee, and caused thee to be fed daily with my angelic food.' *Pseudo-Matthew* gives full accounts of Mary's occupations and miracles (chap. vi.).

[24] Syriac has also twelve years. Some MSS. and the other Gospels have fourteen. According to the latter Mary is invited to marry, but protests her vow of perpetual virginity (*Pseudo-Matthew* vii., viii.; *Nativity* vii.). The high priest says in *Pseudo-Matthew:* 'A new order of life has been found out by Mary alone, who promises that she will remain a virgin to God' (chap. viii.).

[25] 'Each his rod'=staff.

9. And Joseph, throwing away his axe, went out to meet them; and when they had assembled, they went away to the high priest, taking with them their rods. And he, taking the rods of all of them, entered into the temple, and prayed; and having ended his prayer, he took the rods and came out, and gave them to them: but there was no sign in them, and Joseph took his rod last; and, behold, a dove[26] came out of the rod, and flew upon Joseph's head. And the priest said to Joseph, Thou hast been chosen by lot to take into thy keeping the virgin of the Lord. But Joseph refused, saying: I have children, and I am an old man, and she is a young girl. I am afraid lest I become a laughing-stock to the sons of Israel. And the priest said to Joseph: Fear the Lord thy God, and remember what the Lord did to Dathan, and Abiram, and Korah; how the earth opened, and they were swallowed up on account of their contradiction. And now fear, O Joseph, lest the same things happen in thy house. And Joseph was afraid, and took her into his keeping.

---

[26] The dove. The *Nativity of Mary* has a variety. In fulfilment of Isa. 11:1, 2, the successful rod is to produce a flower, on which the Spirit shall settle in the form of a dove. Joseph's rod alone fulfils the condition (chaps. vii., viii.). A prominent feature in pictures of the Marriage of the Virgin by Raphael and his successors is that of the disappointed suitors breaking their useless rods. Mary in the Temple and the Betrothal to Joseph were favourite subjects in the Miracle Plays.

And Joseph said to Mary: Behold, I have received thee from the temple of the Lord; and now I leave thee in my house, and go away to build my buildings, and I shall come to thee. The Lord will protect thee.

Joseph chosen as Mary's Protector

10. And there was a council of the priests, saying: Let us make a veil for the temple of the Lord. And the priest said: Call to me undefiled virgins of the family of David. And the officers went away, and sought, and found seven virgins. And the priest remembered the child Mary, that she was of the family of David, and undefiled before God. And the officers went away and brought her. And they brought them into the temple of the Lord. And the priest said: Choose for me by lot who shall spin the gold, and the white, and the fine linen, and the silk, and the blue,[27] and the scarlet, and the true purple. And the true purple and the scarlet fell to the lot of Mary, and she took them, and went away to her house. And at that time Zacharias was dumb, and Samuel was in his place until the time that Zacharias spake. And Mary took the scarlet, and span it.

---

[27] 'Blue'=hyacinth.

The Annunciation

11. And she took the pitcher, and went out to fill it with water. And, behold, a voice saying: Hail,[28] thou who hast received grace; the Lord is with thee; blessed art thou among women! And she looked round, on the right hand and on the left, to see whence this voice came. And she went away, trembling, to her house, and put down the pitcher; and taking the purple, she sat down on her seat, and drew it out. And, behold, an angel of the Lord stood before her, saying: Fear not, Mary;[29] for thou hast found grace before the Lord of all, and thou[30] shalt conceive, according to His word. And she hearing, reasoned with herself, saying: Shall I conceive by the Lord, the living God? and shall I bring forth as every woman brings forth? And the angel of the Lord said: Not so, Mary; for the power of the Lord shall overshadow thee: wherefore also that holy thing which shall be born of thee shall be called the Son of the Most High. And thou shalt call

---

[28] *Pseudo-Matthew* separates the two annunciations by a day, and makes the first (at the fountain) more distinct (chap. ix.). The *Nativity* has only one (in house, chap. ix.).

[29] This peculiar combination of Matthew and Luke in the address to Mary is found in Justin Martyr (*Apol.* i. 33), from which, with other traits, a use of this Gospel is inferred.

[30] *Lit.*, 'having received joy.' Justin Martyr has again a parallel, 'The Virgin Mary having received grace and joy' (*Dial. with Trypho*, 100).

His name Jesus, for He shall save His people from their sins. And Mary said: Behold, the servant of the Lord before His face: let it be unto me according to thy word.

Mary visits Elizabeth

12. And she made the purple and the scarlet,[31] and took them to the priest. And the priest blessed her, and said: Mary, the Lord God hath magnified thy name, and thou shall be blessed in all the generations of the earth. And Mary, with great joy, went away to Elizabeth her kinswoman, and knocked at the door. And when Elizabeth heard her, she threw away the scarlet, and ran to the door, and opened it; and seeing Mary, she blessed her, and said: Whence is this to me, that the mother of my Lord should come to me? for, behold, that which is in me leaped and blessed thee. But Mary[32] had forgotten the mysteries of which the archangel Gabriel had spoken, and gazed up into heaven, and said: Who am I, O Lord, that all the generations of the earth should bless me? And she remained three months with Elizabeth; and day by day she grew bigger. And Mary being afraid, went away to her own house, and hid herself from the sons

---

[31] 'Scarlet.' The readings vary ('wool,' etc.). Syriac has 'sieve.'
[32] *Cp.* Mary's answer to Joseph below.

of Israel. And she was sixteen years old when these mysteries happened.

13. And she was in her sixth month; and, behold, Joseph came back from his building, and, entering into his house, he discovered that she was big with child. And he smote his face, and threw himself on the ground upon the sackcloth, and wept bitterly, saying: With what face shall I look upon the Lord my God? and what prayer shall I make about this maiden? because I received her a virgin out of the temple of the Lord, and I have not watched over her. Who is it that has hunted me down?[33] Who has done this evil thing in my house, and defiled the virgin? Has not the history of Adam been repeated in me? For just as Adam was in the hour of his[34] singing praise, and the serpent came, and found Eve alone, and completely deceived her, so it has happened to me also. And Joseph stood up from the sackcloth, and called Mary, and said to her: O thou who hast been cared for by God, why hast thou done this, and forgotten the Lord thy God? Why hast thou brought low thy soul, thou that wast brought up in the holy of holies, and that didst receive food from the hand of an

---

[33] Two MSS. read 'hunted *her.*'
[34] In the hour of his 'doxology,' *i.e.*, before the Fall. Some MSS. want or vary this clause.

angel? And she wept bitterly, saying: I am innocent, and have known no man. And Joseph said to her: Whence then is that which is in thy womb? And she said:[35] As the Lord my God liveth, I do not know whence it is to me.

Joseph's Grief over Mary's State

14. And Joseph was greatly afraid, and retired from her, and considered what he should do in regard to her. And Joseph said: If I conceal her sin, I find myself fighting against the law of the Lord; and if I expose her to the sons of Israel, I am afraid lest that which is in her be from an angel,[36] and I shall be found giving up innocent blood to the doom of death. What then shall I do with her? I will put her away from me secretly. And night came upon him; and, behold, an angel of the Lord appears to him in a dream, saying: Be not afraid for this maiden, for that which is in her is of the Holy Spirit; and she will bring forth a Son, and thou shalt call His name Jesus, for He will save His people from their sins. And Joseph arose from sleep, and glorified the God of

---

[35] The answer might truthfully mean that the fact was as great a mystery to Mary herself as to any. But the narrator has already suggested that she had 'forgotten' the mysteries announced by the archangel (chap. xii.)—a clumsy device.

[36] Lit., 'angelic.' In *Pseudo-Matthew* this is the suggestion of the virgins (chap. x.).

Israel, who had given him this grace; and he kept her.

Joseph's & Mary before the Tribunal

15. And Annas the scribe came to him, and said: Why hast thou not appeared in our assembly? And Joseph said to him: Because I was weary from my journey, and rested the first day. And he turned, and saw that Mary was with child. And he ran away to the priest, and said to him: Joseph, whom thou didst vouch for, has committed a grievous crime. And the priest said: How so? And he said: He has defiled the virgin whom he received out of the temple of the Lord, and has married her by stealth, and has not revealed it to the sons of Israel. And the priest answering, said: Has Joseph done this? Then said Annas the scribe: Send officers, and thou wilt find the virgin with child. And the officers went away, and found it as he had said; and they brought her along with Joseph to the tribunal. And the priest said: Mary, why hast thou done this? and why hast thou brought thy soul low, and forgotten the Lord thy God? Thou that wast reared in the holy of holies, and that didst receive food from the hand of an angel, and didst hear the hymns, and didst dance before Him, why hast thou done this? And she wept bitterly, saying: As the Lord my God liveth, I am pure

before Him, and know not a man. And the priest said to Joseph: Why hast thou done this? And Joseph said: As the Lord liveth, I am pure concerning her. Then said the priest: Bear not false witness, but speak the truth. Thou hast married her by stealth, and hast not revealed it to the sons of Israel, and hast not bowed thy head under the strong hand, that thy seed might be blessed. And Joseph was silent.

They drink the Water of the Ordeal

16. And the priest said: Give up the virgin whom thou didst receive out of the temple of the Lord. And Joseph burst into tears. And the priest said: I will give you to drink of the water[37] of the ordeal of the Lord, and He shall make manifest your sins in your eyes. And the priest took the water, and gave Joseph to drink, and sent him away to the hill-country; and he returned unhurt. And he gave to Mary also to drink, and sent her away to the hill-country; and she returned unhurt. And all the people wondered that sin did not appear in them. And the priest

---

[37] The water of jealousy (Numb. 5). It need not be said that there is no warrant in law or custom for the application of this ordeal to men. In the *Protevangelium* Joseph and Mary are sent to the hill-country and return unhurt; in *Pseudo-Matthew* they walk round the altar seven times, and are cleansed on the spot (chap. xii.). The Trial of Joseph and Mary was another favourite subject of the Mediæval Mysteries.

said: If the Lord God has not made manifest your sins, neither do I judge you. And he sent them away. And Joseph took Mary, and went away to his own house, rejoicing and glorifying the God of Israel.

Joseph & Mary journey to Bethlehem

17. And there was an order from the Emperor Augustus, that all in Bethlehem of Judea should be enrolled. And Joseph said: I shall enrol my sons, but what shall I do with this maiden? How shall I enrol her? As my wife? I am ashamed. As my daughter then? But all the sons of Israel know that she is not my daughter. The day of the Lord shall itself bring it to pass as the Lord will. And he saddled the ass, and set her upon it; and his son led it, and Joseph followed. And when they had come within three miles, Joseph turned and saw her sorrowful; and he said to himself: Likely that which is in her distresses her. And again Joseph turned and saw her laughing. And he said to her: Mary, how is it that I see in thy face at one time laughter, at another sorrow? And Mary said to Joseph: Because I see two peoples with my eyes; the one weeping and lamenting, and the other rejoicing and exulting. And they came into the middle of the road, and Mary said to him: Take me down from off the ass, for that which is in me presses to come forth. And he took her

down from off the ass, and said to her: Whither shall I lead thee, and cover thy disgrace? for the place is desert.

18. And he found a cave there, and led her into it;[38] and leaving his two sons beside her, he went out to seek a midwife in the district of Bethlehem.

Miraculous Occurrences on the Way

And I Joseph was walking, and was not walking;[39] and I looked up into the sky, and saw the sky astonished; and I looked up to the pole of the heavens, and saw it standing, and the birds of the air keeping still. And I looked down upon

---

[38] The birth of Jesus in a cave is a very early tradition, and seems to have some local origin. Justin mentions it (*Dial. with Trypho*, 78); and Origen says, 'There is shown at Bethlehem the cave where He was born, and the manger in the cave where He was wrapped in swaddling-clothes' (*Against Celsus*, I. 51). Jerome repeatedly mentions it: 'That cave in which the Son of God was born,' 'that venerable cave,' etc. (*Cp.* letters to Sabianus and Paulinus). It is to be noticed, however, that in the apocryphal story (1) the cave is situated about three miles from Bethlehem (Mary being overtaken by childbirth in the way); and (2) the stable is not in the cave, but is sought some days after (chap. xxii.; *Pseudo-Matthew* xiv.; thus also Justin). There is no certain basis for the tradition.

[39] The narrative here (chap. xviii.) changes to the first person (Joseph being now the speaker), and from comparative sobriety becomes wildly fantastic. It is plain that in this chapter we are dealing with another and older source—probably with part of the original Gospel. This leads to the suspicion, strengthened by what follows, that the Gospel took its origin in Esseno-Ebionitic or early Gnostic circles.

the earth, and saw a trough lying, and work-people reclining: and their hands were in the trough. And those that were eating did not eat, and those that were rising did not carry it up, and those that were conveying anything to their mouths did not convey it; but the faces of all were looking upwards. And I saw the sheep walking, and the sheep stood still; and the shepherd raised his hand to strike them, and his hand remained up. And I looked upon the current of the river, and I saw the mouths of the kids resting on the water and not drinking, and all things in a moment were driven from their course.

19. And I saw a woman coming down from the[40] hill-country, and she said to me: O man, whither art thou going? And I said: I am seeking an Hebrew midwife. And she answered and said unto me: Art thou of Israel? And I said to her: Yes. And she said: And who is it that is bringing forth in the cave? And I said: A woman betrothed to me. And she said to me: Is she not thy wife?

---

[40] The story of the midwives and of the Nativity in the cave is again a favourite subject with the Mediæval Mystery-writers. It cannot be overlooked that in the story the birth of Jesus is robbed of part of its reality. Jesus is not born after the manner of other children. A great light fills the cave, and, as it decreases, the infant Jesus appears, while His mother remains a virgin. There is thus a docetic tinge in the narrative. This bears out the above suggestion of its origin.

And I said to her: It is Mary that was reared in the temple of the Lord, and I obtained her by lot as my wife. And yet she is not my wife, but has conceived of the Holy Spirit.

Birth of Jesus

And the midwife said to him: Is this true? And Joseph said to her: Come and see. And the midwife went away with him. And they stood in the place of the cave, and behold a luminous cloud overshadowed the cave. And the midwife said: My soul has been magnified this day, because mine eyes have seen strange things— because salvation has been brought forth to Israel. And immediately the cloud disappeared out of the cave, and a great light shone in the cave, so that the eyes could not bear it. And in a little that light gradually decreased, until the infant appeared, and went and took the breast from his mother Mary. And the midwife cried out, and said: This is a great day to me, because I have seen this strange sight. And the midwife went forth out of the cave, and Salome met her. And she said to her: Salome, Salome, I have a strange sight to relate to thee: a virgin has brought forth—a thing which her nature admits not of. Then said Salome: As the Lord my God liveth, unless I thrust in my finger, and search the parts I will not believe that a virgin has brought forth.

20. And the midwife went in, and said to Mary: Show thyself; for no small controversy has arisen about thee. And Salome put in her finger, and cried out, and said: Woe is me for mine iniquity and mine unbelief, because I have tempted the living God; and, behold, my hand is dropping off as if burned with fire. And she bent her knees before the Lord, saying: O God of my fathers, remember that I am the seed of Abraham, and Isaac, and Jacob; do not make a show of me to the sons of Israel, but restore me to the poor; for Thou knowest, O Lord, that in Thy name I have performed my services, and that I have received my reward at Thy hand. And, behold, an angel of the Lord stood by her, saying to her: Salome, Salome, the Lord hath heard thee. Put thy hand to the infant, and carry it, and thou wilt have safety and joy. And Salome went and carried it, saying: I will worship Him, because a great King has been born to Israel. And, behold, Salome was immediately cured, and she went forth out of the cave justified. And behold a voice saying: Salome, Salome, tell not the strange things thou hast seen, until the child has come into Jerusalem.

Salome's Punishment and Cure

21. And, behold, Joseph was ready to go into Judea. And there was a great commotion in Bethlehem of Judea, for Magi came, saying: Where is he that is born king of the Jews? for we have seen his star in the east, and have come to worship him. And when Herod heard, he was much disturbed, and sent officers to the Magi. And he sent for the priests, and examined them, saying: How is it written about the Christ? where is He to be born? And they said: In Bethlehem of Judea, for so it is written. And he sent them away. And he examined the Magi, saying to them: What sign have you seen in reference to the king that has been born? And the Magi said: We have seen a star of great size shining among these stars, and obscuring their light, so that the stars did not appear; and we thus knew that a king has been born to Israel, and we have come to worship him. And Herod said: Go and seek him; and if you find him, let me know, in order that I also may go and worship him. And the Magi went out. And, behold, the star which they had seen in the east went before them until they came to the cave, and it stood over the top of the cave. And the Magi saw the infant with His mother Mary; and they brought forth from their bag gold, and frankincense, and myrrh. And having been warned by the angel not to go into

Judea, they went into their own country by another road.

Visit of the Magi

22. And when Herod knew that he had been mocked by the Magi, in a rage he sent murderers, saying to them: Slay the children from two years old and under. And Mary, having heard that the children were being killed, was afraid, and took the infant and swaddled Him, and put Him into an oxstall.[41] And Elizabeth, having heard that they were searching for John, took him and went up into the hill-country, and kept looking where to conceal him. And there was no place of concealment. And Elizabeth, groaning with a loud voice, says: O mountain of God, receive mother and child. And immediately the mountain was cleft, and received her. And a light shone about them, for an angel of the Lord was with them, watching over them.

Murder of Zacharias

23. And Herod searched for John, and sent officers to Zacharias, saying: Where hast thou hid thy son? And he, answering, said to them: I am the servant of God in holy things, and I sit

---

[41] *Pseudo-Matthew* (chap. xiv.) brings in the well-known trait of the ox and the ass adoring Christ in the stall, in supposed fulfilment of Isa. 1:3.

constantly in the temple of the Lord: I do not know where my son is. And the officers went away, and reported all these things to Herod. And Herod was enraged, and said: His son is destined to be king over Israel. And he sent to him again, saying: Tell the truth; where is thy son? for thou knowest that thy life is in my hand. And Zacharias said: I am God's martyr, if thou sheddest my blood; for the Lord will receive my spirit, because thou sheddest innocent blood at the vestibule of the temple of the Lord. And Zacharias[42] was murdered about daybreak. And the sons of Israel did not know that he had been murdered.

24. But at the hour of the salutation the priests went away, and Zacharias did not come forth to meet them with a blessing, according to his custom. And the priests stood waiting for Zacharias to salute him at the prayer, and to glorify the Most High. And he still delaying, they were all afraid. But one of them ventured to go in, and he saw clotted blood beside the altar; and he heard a voice saying: Zacharias has been

---

[42] The episode of the death of Zacharias, the father of the Baptist, is not found in the other Apocryphal Gospels, but may have been part of the original of this. It is evidently evolved from Christ's allusion to the murder of Zacharias in Matt. 23:35 (*Cp.* 2 Chron. 24:21). The cleaving of the mountain to receive Elizabeth and her babe is of the type of the marvels that precede.

murdered, and his blood shall not be wiped up until his avenger come. And hearing this saying, he was afraid, and went out and told it to the priests. And they ventured in, and saw what had happened; and the fretwork of the temple made a wailing noise, and they rent their clothes from the top even to the bottom. And they found not his body, but they found his blood turned into stone. And they were afraid, and went out and reported to the people that Zacharias had been murdered. And all the tribes of the people heard, and mourned, and lamented for him three days and three nights. And after the three days, the priests consulted as to whom they should put in his place; and the lot fell upon Simeon. For it was he who had been warned by the Holy Spirit that he should not see death until he should see the Christ in the flesh.

25. And I James[43] that wrote this history in Jerusalem, a commotion having arisen when Herod died, withdrew myself to the wilderness until the commotion in Jerusalem ceased, glorifying the Lord God, who had given me the gift and the wisdom to write this history. And grace shall be with them that fear our Lord Jesus Christ, to whom be glory to ages of ages. Amen.

---

[43] The James intended is no doubt the Lord's brother, who figures also in the *Clementines* and other pseudo-graphic compositions.

About CrossReach Publications

Thank you for choosing <u>CrossReach Publications</u>.

Our philosophy is to remain as neutral as possible. We are non-denominational and non-sectarian. We seek to publish books from a wide variety of authors and doctrinal positions, on a wide variety of Christian topics that will teach, encourage, challenge, inspire and equip. We appreciate and respect what every part of the body brings to the table and believe everyone has the right to study and come to their own conclusions. *We aim to help to facilitate that end.*

We aspire to excellence. If we have not met your standards please contact us and let us know. We want you to feel satisfied with your product. Amy, our 11 year old, has recently joined the business now and is publishing her own books. And Sarah, our 5 year old, loves to mimic daddy "doing the books"!

We're a family-based home-business. A husband and wife team raising 8 kids. You can see us in action in our family vlog. If you have any questions or comments about our publications or our channel you can do so by emailing us.

www.YouTube.com/c/TheKinsellaBunchVlog
CrossReach@outlook.com

Don't forget you can follow us on <u>Facebook</u> and <u>Twitter</u>, and keep up to date on our newest releases and deals.

More Apocrypha & Pseudepigrapha Titles

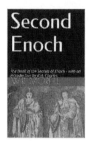

<u>Second Enoch</u>
W. R. Morfil

Includes an introduction by R.H. Charles, famed translator of the 1st Book of Enoch. This book makes up part of what is now known as the Old Testament Pseudepigrapha. It will be of major interest to students of ancient religion, Judaism, early Christianity and more.

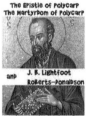

<u>The Epistle of Polycarp to the Philippians and the Martyrdom of Polycarp</u>
J. B. Lightfoot

THE Epistle is usually made a sort of preface to those of Ignatius, for reasons which will be obvious to the reader. Yet he was born later, and lived to a much later period. They seem to have been friends from the days of their common pupilage under St. John; and there is nothing improbable in the conjecture of Usher, that he was the "angel of the church in Smyrna," to whom the Master says, "Be thou faithful unto death, and I will give thee a crown of life." His pupil Irenaeus gives us one of the very few portraits of an apostolic man which are to be found in antiquity, in a few sentences which are a picture: "I could describe the very place in which the blessed Polycarp sat and taught; his going out and coming in; the whole tenor of his life; his personal appearance; how he would speak of the conversations he had held with John and with others who had seen the Lord. How did he make mention of their words and of whatever he had heard from them respecting the Lord." Thus he unconsciously tantalizes our reverent curiosity. Alas! that such conversations were not written for our learning. But there is a wise Providence in what is withheld, as well as in the inestimable treasures we have received.

THE Martyrdom purports to have been written by the church at Smyrna to the church at Philomelium, and through that church to the whole Christian world, in order to give a succinct account of the circumstances attending the martyrdom of Polycarp. It is the earliest of all the Martyria, and has generally been accounted both the most interesting and authentic. Not a few, however, deem it interpolated in several passages, and some refer it to a much later date than the middle of the second century, to which it has been commonly ascribed. We cannot tell how much it may owe to the writers who successively transcribed it. Great part of it has been engrossed by Eusebius in his Ecclesiastical History (iv. 15); and it is instructive to observe, that some of the most startling miraculous phenomena recorded in the text as it now stands, have no place in the narrative as given by that early historian of the church. Much discussion has arisen respecting several particulars contained in this Martyrium; but into these disputes we do not enter, having it for our aim simply to present the reader with as faithful a translation as possible of this very interesting monument of Christian antiquity.

The Apocryphal Third Epistle of Paul to the Corinthians: or 3 Corinthians
M. R. James

This epistle, often considered one of the forgotten, forbidden or lost books of the Bible is purported to be the third of three letters to the Corinthians by the Apostle Paul. While the canonical epistles are regarded almost unanimously as genuine writings of the renowned New Testament writer, this writing is universally rejected as pseudepigraphal. In saying that it was accepted as canonical in some parts of the East at various times during the middle ages.

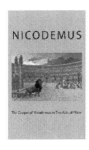

NICODEMUS

The Gospel of Nicodemus or The Acts of Pilate

Although this Gospel is, by some among the learned, supposed to have been really written by Nicodemus, who became a disciple of Jesus Christ, and conversed with him; others conjecture that it was a forgery towards the close of the third century by some zealous believer, who observing that there had been appeals made by the Christians of the former age, to the Acts of Pilate, but that such Acts could not be produced, imagined it would be of service to Christianity to fabricate and publish this Gospel; as it would both confirm the Christians under persecution, and convince the Heathens of the truth of the Christian religion. The Rev. Jeremiah Jones says, that such pious frauds were very common among Christians even in the first three centuries; and that a forgery of this nature, with the view above mentioned, seems natural and probable. The same author, in noticing that Eusebius, in his Ecclesiastical history, charges the Pagans with having forged and published a book, called "The Acts of Pilate," takes occasion to observe, that the internal evidence of this Gospel shows it was not the work of any Heathen; but that if in the latter end of the third century we find it in use among Christians (as it was then certainly in some churches) and about the same time find a forgery of the Heathens under the same title, it seems exceedingly probable that some Christians, at that time, should publish such a piece as this, in order partly to confront the spurious one of the Pagans, and partly to support those appeals which had been made by former Christians to the Acts of Pilate; and Mr. Jones says, he thinks so more particularly as we have innumerable instances of forgeries by the faithful in the primitive ages, grounded on less plausible reasons. Whether it be canonical or not, it is of very great antiquity, and is appealed to by several of the ancient Christians.

The Shepherd of Hermas
J. B. Lightfoot

The Shepherd of Hermas is an astounding piece of ancient Christian writing. It is usually dated at between 120 Ad and 150 Ad. This means that the author may have been in contact with an Apostle such as John who died around 98 Ad. And he was most certainly contemporaneous with those who knew some of the Apostle such as Ignatius and Polycarp.

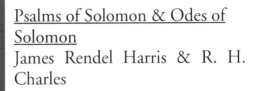

Psalms of Solomon & Odes of Solomon
James Rendel Harris & R. H. Charles

In the Odes we have few quotations or adaptations from previous writings, whether Jewish or Christian; there is little that can be traced to the Old Testament, almost nothing that is to be credited to the Gospels or other branches of the Christian literature. Their radiance is no reflection from the illumination of other days: their inspiration is first-hand and immediate; it answers very well to the summary which Aristides made of the life of the early Christian Church when he described them as indeed 'a new people with whom something Divine is mingled.' They are thus altogether distinct from the extant Psalms of Solomon.

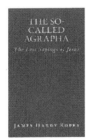

The So-Called Agrapha: The Lost Sayings of Jesus
James Hardy Ropes

To know a little more of the life of Christ, whether of his works or words, than the tradition embodied in the gospels tells has from early times been the eager desire of men. Apocryphal books almost without number have one after another held the attention of great numbers of Christians, only to be recognized in the end as disappointing fictions. One line of serious investigation, however, has been followed persistently and hopefully—the search for scattered sayings of the Lord preserved outside of the canonical gospels, the so-called Agrapha. One of these is familar to all, the word quoted in Paul's speech at Miletus, Acts 20:35, and was early noticed. That the writings of the Fathers contain others which may have claims to genuineness was also seen centuries ago, and the great patristic editors of the seventeenth and eighteenth centuries collected in their notes much valuable material bearing on the subject. Collections of the sayings themselves were also made, and under various names (among which that of "Agrapha" seems first to occur in 1776) have been current ever since Grabe published in 1698 in his Spicilegium eleven Dicta Jesu Christi quæ in IV. Evangeliis non extant. Of recent collections of the more important Agrapha, R. Hofmann's, in his Leben Jesu nach den Apokryphen, Westcott's, in his Introduction to the Study of the Gospels, and Schaff's, in the first volume of his History of the Christian Church, are easily accessible and convenient examples. These and similar collections have generally contained from twenty to thirty sayings, and have been largely dependent on the lists of Grabe and Fabricius.

The 400 Silent Years: from Malachi to Matthew
H. A. Ironside

Fully illustrated. Includes all of the drawings from the original edition. What is the history between the Old and New Testaments? Most people are not even aware there is such a gap. But there is. A 400 year gap. When the Old Testament leaves off the Jews have just returned back from Babylonian captivity and the Persian Empire is in full swing. When Jesus enters the scene it is 400 years later. The Persians are long gone, the Greeks have had their time and now the Romans rule to roost. So what happened? Do we have any writings from this time? Could understanding this period of time help us understand the New Testament, the world of Jesus and the Apostles? The answer is yes. This exciting book by well-known author H. A. Ironside lifts the veil from this vital period of Jewish history and helps piece together the events that brought them from Malachi to Matthew. This book will be of interest to students of

Biblical, Ancient Near Eastern, Greek and Roman history as well as all those who desire to know and understand the Bible for fully.

The Epistle of Barnabas
Kirsopp Lake

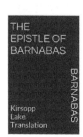

The document which is always known as the Epistle of Barnabas is, like 1st Clement, really anonymous, and it is generally regarded as impossible to accept the tradition which ascribes it to the Barnabas who was a companion of S. Paul, though it is convenient to continue to use the title.

It is either a general treatise or was intended for some community in which Alexandrian ideas prevailed, though it is not possible to define either its destination, or the locality from which it was written, with any greater accuracy. Its main object is to warn Christians against a Judaistic conception of the Old Testament, and the writer carries a symbolic exegesis as far as did Philo; indeed he goes farther and apparently denies any literal significance at all to the commands of the Law. The literal exegesis of the ceremonial law is to him a device of an evil angel who deceived the Jews.

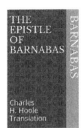

The Epistle of Barnabas
Charles H. Hoole

WE owe to the discovery of the Codex Sinaiticus the Greek text of the epistle of St. Barnabas.1 In that manuscript it comes at the end of the New Testament, between the Book of Revelation and the Shepherd of Hernias, with which the manuscript concludes, The heading is simply the Epistle of Barnabas, and the title is repeated at the end. Previous to the discovery of this manuscript, though a considerable portion of the Greek remained, chapters 1-4 were lost, and the epistle was known chiefly by an ancient Latin version, which is itself imperfect, the three concluding chapters being lost ; the portion which remained in Greek furnished only a very inferior text, and the epistle could not consequently be read in a state which would assure us that we had the work in the same shape as it presented in the Ante-Nicene period.

Made in the USA
Monee, IL
05 November 2019